RETIRE EARLY

The Complete Guide on How to Retire Early and Live Stress-Free over the Long Term

BY

ANTHONY HESTON

Table of Contents

INTRODUCTION

I want to thank you and congratulate you for downloading the book *"Retire Early: The Complete Guide on How to Retire Early and Live Stress-Free over the Long Term."*

This book contains some basic information about life after retirement as well as proven steps and strategies on how to plan for the time when you will no longer be working every day purely to make a living.

Entering into retirement is a huge step in any person's life. Unfortunately, a lot of people today do not realize the importance of preparing for one's retirement. They are often too focused on working to make money to afford to fulfill their needs in the present that they neglect to set aside time to even think about being financially secure in their later years. As a result, they are likely to end up unprepared for a future when they are no longer able to work as full-time salary-earning professionals yet still have to somehow pay the bills.

You can prevent this nightmare from ever happening to you by reading and understanding what this book can teach you. Through the lessons discussed herein, you will have a better idea of how you can prepare for your eventual retirement so that you can have as few hassles as possible while enjoying your permanent break after all the years you spent as a full-time working professional—a break that you so rightfully deserve.

This book hopes to impart upon its readers, especially the younger professionals out there, the knowledge that they need to make sound decisions regarding their finances, their health, and other important matters that have a big impact in their future. This is to minimize the time and effort they spend performing "damage control" and more time reaping the benefits of all their years of hard work.

Remember, retirement is a time when you should be taking it easy and enjoying the remaining years of your life, not a period of constant frustration and anxiety. Preparing for it will require a lot of effort on your part, but in the end, it is you and your family who will benefit from it the most.

Thanks again for downloading this book! I hope you enjoy it!

CHAPTER 1

RETIREMENT PLANNING EXPLAINED

If you're reading this book, it's probably because you want to know how to make sure you'll be all set to live a comfortable life by the time you stop working full-time, whether you're your own boss or employed by somebody else. The reality is that, even if you want to keep on working to continue earning money for the rest of your life, old age and the things that come with it can hinder your ability to pursue that option. Your physical and mental dexterity will naturally deteriorate over time because of the way the human body was put together. This will inevitably make you less and less capable of doing the things you do every day, even those that are not related to what you do for a living, no matter how much you want to stay active.

Moreover, even if you feel that you can still take on any job after you have reached old age, companies will almost always prioritize younger people as they have more years ahead of them to devote to their work. Of course, this is not much of a concern if you are self-employed or managing your own business, in which case you can keep on working as long as you want. However, if you do not belong to this category, you should start thinking about how you will fare when you are asked to make way for "new blood" in the organization to which you belong. You might have a hard time trying to convince your employer that you will continue to be the right person for the job in the years to come. If you still want to keep on working, you might end up with a job that will not match your qualifications or one with much lower pay compared to what you were earning before.

If you have children who are fortunate enough to become working professionals themselves, they can set aside part of their income to support you in your retirement. However, your children are also likely to have children of their own—children that they need to raise and support in the same way that you raised and supported yours. It might not set a good example for them if you rely on them to shoulder even some of your retirement expenses when they should be more concerned with making sure their own families will always have food on the table. Otherwise, you run the risk of putting into motion a vicious cycle that could lead to all sorts of problems for your family.

The good news is there is a way for you to be financially secure and not become dependent on anyone else by the time you enter that great stage of life called retirement. With proper planning, good judgment, and the right state of mind, you can have enough savings that you can spend on all the things you need even if you will no longer be getting a steady paycheck every month. After all, for as long as you are still living and breathing, you will still need some essential items to make your life easier, and just about every one of those items does not come for free.

In a nutshell, retirement planning isn't simply planning for what you'll do when you retire; it's making sure you will have enough money to spend on the things you and your family will need after you retire.

The right time to start planning for your retirement

Planning for your retirement should start at the earliest possible time, not when the time to retire is already fast approaching, and certainly not when you're already retired! This is because making sure you will not be wanting in the future involves a lot of preparation in the present. It is no small matter to do all that is necessary in the present to be guaranteed of steady income and other benefits by the time you are no longer making a living. This is especially important if you are the breadwinner in your family and there are people who still depend on you because they are not yet capable of supporting themselves, such as your children.

With that being said, this book was written primarily for young twentysomething or thirtysomething professionals who are still years away from the age at which they choose to officially leave the workforce, whether it's at 65 or earlier. However, older people who have not yet done any actual planning for their retirement should not despair. Retirement planning will be especially challenging for someone who has had a late start in the race (as it is not likely that a few short years of preparation will yield steady income of a substantial amount later on), but it is not impossible for that person to come up with a doable plan with the end goal of earning enough to pay for their future needs as well as the needs of their family. In fact, the last chapter of this book is all about helping people plan for retirement in case it is just around the corner instead of decades away.

At the very least, coming up with a plan for your retirement very late in the game is still better than not coming up with a plan at all.

The right time to retire

The typical age of retirement in the United States is 65 as it is often around this age that people truly feel their bodies are no longer capable of functioning as well as they used to. Even something as simple as walking up a flight of stairs can become a challenge for someone of that age. You can thus can imagine just how hard it is for that same person to be working for a living for eight to nine hours five days a week, even if their job is not too physically demanding.

Somewhat surprisingly, there is a steadily growing number of people who voluntarily retire from the workforce every year despite not yet reaching the age of sixty. A minority have opted to do so even while still in their forties, which implies that the decision to retire need not be dictated by a person's age or whether or not they are still capable of working full-time.

In any case, the decision as to when you will retire rests only with you (provided you are fortunate enough not to have figured in an accident which will lead to you being medically retired with full disability benefits). However, if you are thinking of retiring well before you reach the national standard of 65, you first need to deliberate whether or not you can afford to live a comfortable life without the benefit of your present salary.

If you are a young professional, you will have a much better chance of being financially secure in your retirement if you will continue to work for as long as you are able to do so. The biggest chunk of what will go into your retirement savings is expected to come from your regular salary (or your profit if you are an entrepreneur). Hence, the more money you make in the present, the more money will go into your savings for the future.

Determining the amount of money you'll need for your retirement

Before you start planning where you will get your total retirement fund, it pays to have a rough idea of how much the fund will need to be by the time you will begin directly benefiting from it. Bloomberg.com, CNN.com, and other legitimate news and financial websites have calculators for determining this figure to relieve you of some of the hassle of doing the numbers by yourself. Some calculators even account for projected inflation to give you an idea of what the purchasing power of your money will be several years from now, though this number shouldn't be treated as absolute in light of the many variables that can affect inflation.

You shouldn't worry too much either if the numbers you come up with seem somewhat unrealistic to you even after you have done the math plenty of times. After all, you will never truly know whether or not you have saved enough money for your retirement until the time comes when you will actually be needing that money. In any case, making projections as early as now and regularly reassessing your finances will give you a measure of comfort as well as a means of gauging your progress in saving up for your retirement. It can also help prevent the nightmare of finding out just as you are about to retire that you don't have enough savings.

Relevance to estate planning

If you still believe that retirement planning is unnecessary because you feel you have amassed a great wealth over the years or because you'd rather let fate take its course and trust that she will show you some mercy, perhaps this hypothetical scenario will change your mind.

You are the breadwinner in your family. You reach old age with nothing to your name except money in the bank and a few personal belongings. You die suddenly and unexpectedly, but that is only the first of the many problems that your family will face when you're gone. Because you didn't leave behind anything else that they could fall back on, your spouse is forced to sell all the assets that are in your name just so that your family will have food to eat, clothes to wear, and a roof over their heads. There is no guarantee as to how long those things will last, and with your assets already sold, your family is likely to incur huge debts just so they could still enjoy the barest of necessities.

Do you still think retirement planning is just a waste of time? Can you still sleep soundly at night knowing that the aforementioned scenario could be your financial legacy to your family? When the time comes for you to depart from this world, will you be happy knowing that your spouse and children become more and more miserable because of the mess you left them?

If for nothing else, retirement planning helps make sure that your estate planning efforts will go smoothly. If you're not that concerned with making sure you yourself will have enough savings when you retire, you should at least make sure your family, especially your children, will have enough to live on even several years after your passing.

CHAPTER 2

THE INEVITABLE FINANCIAL GAP

When you think of income, the first thing that would come to your mind is your current salary. It is essentially the money in your name that: 1) is of a substantial amount and 2) keeps on growing (provided you are wise enough to put some of it into your savings). Obviously, you cannot start saving any money for future use unless it continually flows into what constitutes your budget.

Of course, the amount on the paycheck you receive at the end of the month will still undergo a lot of changes before it can finally be something that you can set aside for later. You still have to pay your taxes like any good citizen should, and you have to spend on daily living essentials like food, clothing, health care, the place you live in (by paying either rent or mortgage), water, and electricity just to name a few. With how much all these things cost these days, you will definitely feel the pinch whenever they take a big bite out of your budget. Add to that your obligation to pay any debts that you may have incurred, which can further trim down your existing funds.

The money that is left after you have paid for all of the above necessities is known as your disposable income. This is the money that you can spend on whatever you want without having to explain yourself to anyone (except maybe your spouse). You are free to decide how you will spend this money, but for the sake of prudence, it would be best if you set aside at least some of it for a rainy day.

Assuming you keep on working at your present job until the day you retire not just from your company but from the entire workforce as well, chances are the disposable income you will have upon your retirement won't be enough to pay for all your needs even if you put every single penny of it into your savings account, which would likely have a rather low interest rate of only 0.06% (the national average for 2016). Remember that your disposable income is the money that remains in your name after you have spent on some of the things that you need for daily living. If you will rely on nothing but your disposable income in the present to cover all your daily living needs in the future, you can expect your finances to fall well short of your projected total expenses.

And when you add inflation to the mix, the purchasing power of your savings will keep on shrinking through the years, leaving a much wider gap between what you have when you retire and what you need to spend on then. Social security will be there to shoulder specific expenses and thus serve as a kind of "safety net," but you are not allowed to benefit from it in any way unless you are 70 years of age or physically disabled as a result of your line of work. Also, it can never become a readily available source of substantial funds that you can use anytime for just about anything.

You clearly need to do something about this gap before it finally rears its ugly head, and the best time to do something about it is *right now*. Fortunately, help is readily available to those who are willing to learn.

Filling the gap

One good thing about retirement planning is that you need not depend on only one source of income to build what will serve as your "nest egg" for the years following your official departure from the workforce. You may choose from a wide selection of benefit and investment instruments that can exponentially boost your retirement savings beyond what your disposable income alone can provide.

The next three chapters of this book will discuss these essentials in detail so that you will know how to get the most out of them before and after you retire.

CHAPTER 3

SAVING UP FOR YOUR RETIREMENT

You can have a steady source of funds to serve as your retirement savings without having to touch your disposable income. If you belong to the regular workforce, chances are you've already heard of these types of accounts.

Defined Contribution Plan

This is a type of retirement savings plan wherein a certain percentage or amount of money is periodically deposited to an interest-earning savings account that has special restrictions. Such restrictions are in place to discourage premature withdrawals, hence giving the fund the opportunity to grow into a hefty amount by the time it may be withdrawn.

A defined contribution plan is not the same as a regular salary in that the funds will become available only at a later time and not instantaneously. However, both involve payouts wherein the employee will benefit directly.

Here are the two main types of defined contribution plans being implemented today:

1.   The 401(k) Plan

A 401(k) plan is often the first thing that comes to people's minds whenever the topic of retirement savings is discussed.

The 401(k) plans are government-sanctioned retirement accounts. They are named after subsection 401(k) of the Internal Revenue Code, which states (among other things) that an employee of a company has the option of having the latter make regular contributions to a trust plan under the former's name as a form of profit-sharing.

Under this plan, however, it is not just your employer who makes periodic contributions to your 401(k) account. You will be making periodic contributions as well, and these contributions are usually taken from your salary before any taxes are deducted. Upon your retirement, you can withdraw the ending total amount of the fund plus any earnings it has generated over time.

Whenever your employer reports your taxable salary to the IRS, the resulting amount does not include the contributions you have made to your 401(k) account. All the money you contribute to your account is tax-deferred, which means anything you earn in the form of returns on your contributions will become taxable only at a later date instead of as soon as such returns are generated. Because you will pay taxes only when you withdraw from your account upon your retirement, leaving the principal untouched can lead to it being reinvested over and over. This allows the combined amount to keep on compounding to give you a much bigger fund value than what is otherwise possible.

Moreover, you have full discretion on how the money that accumulates in your account is to be invested. The plan will provide you with a selection of investments (More on the different types of investments will be discussed in the succeeding chapter.), and you need to be well informed to know which of the available investments will be most effective in helping you achieve financial security and your other long-term goals.

Participating in a 401(k) plan won't be a problem as Federal law requires all private businesses to give their employees the option to enroll in the plan once they become eligible to do so. As is the case in many organizations, an employee must be at least 21 years of age and must have rendered at least 1,000 work hours over a 12-month period to become eligible.

One drawback with the 401(k) plan is that the amount of funds you will have upon your retirement will be based on the market value of the account (which will depend on the performance of your chosen investments), not necessarily on the number of contributions and the amount of each contribution. As such, you may receive a payout that is less than what you may have come up with during your earlier calculations.

On the other hand, if you will keep making wise investment decisions over the years, your 401(k) could end up comprising the bulk of your nest egg.

The returns generated could even possibly provide you with an effective hedge or counter to inflation. Still, it's best not to get too excited and simply rely on your 401(k) alone to save the day. You should make it a point to exhaust all possible savings and investment options before focusing on only a few.

2.   Individual Retirement Accounts

As mentioned in the preceding paragraph, one concern about the 401(k) plan is that the payout you will receive upon your retirement is not of a guaranteed figure despite your contributions being defined at the moment you deposited each one of them into the fund. The good news is that there are alternatives that will enable you to get the full amount of your principal back as well as any interest incurred. These alternative retirement savings accounts are called individual retirement accounts (IRAs).

Whereas 401(k) plans are limited to those who work for organizations that offer such plans, IRAs are typically open to anyone provided they have not yet reached the age of seventy and a half.

Also, unlike in a 401(k) plan, every single penny that goes into an IRA will come from your money alone. You are free to withdraw from the contributions you made to the IRA (but not on their earnings) even before your retirement and not incur any taxes or penalties as it is not a government-sanctioned account, unlike a 401(k). As such, you can open an IRA through a bank, a brokerage firm, a federally insured credit union, or a mutual fund company for as long as it has received approval from the IRS to offer such accounts to interested individuals.

There are two types of IRAs—traditional IRAs and Roth IRAs:

a. A *traditional IRA* is similar to a 401(k) in that you will get taxed only when you withdraw the principal amount as well as any generated interest when you retire, hence allowing the fund to grow substantially thanks to compounding.

b. The *Roth IRA* is named after William Roth, a US Senator from Delaware who co-sponsored the law that led to its implementation (the Taxpayer Relief Act of 1997). In a Roth IRA, any contributions you make to it are not tax-deductible as they are already taken from your post-tax income. However, all withdrawals you make from the account will be tax-free. Also, the Roth IRA allows you to make contributions even after you reach the age of seventy and a half for as long as you continue to earn income.

IRAs also have drawbacks, though. An account holder can make regular contributions of no more than $5,000 if aged 49 or younger and no more than $6,000 if aged 50 or older. This may not seem much at first glance, but for those who have opened IRAs much later in life, this setup has little chance of yielding a significant return in time for retirement.

Financial planners recommend that working professionals have both a 401(k) plan and an IRA of any type. Although it could mean a much lower disposable income in the present, the tradeoff is bigger savings and more capital gains that you can use when you retire. Thus, you shouldn't feel you're simply depriving yourself of your hard-earned money in the here and now. You can enjoy all of it—

and more (i.e. gains)—when you're no longer working full-time.

Defined Benefit Plan

A defined benefit plan, also known as a pension plan, is an option wherein a company provides its employees with a pre-established or "defined" benefit upon retirement. It is not the figure itself that is defined. Rather, it is the formula used in computing the final total payout that is defined and therefore cannot be modified. Computing for a defined benefit payout will take into account the number of years you have worked for an employer that offers such a plan as well as your salary.

Unlike in a defined contribution plan, the total benefit to which you are entitled under a defined benefit plan will not be available to you all at once as soon as you retire. You will instead receive it in the form of regular payments throughout your life starting from the time you officially leave the workforce.

The number of organizations that offer defined benefit plans in the United States have gradually been dwindling every year ever since it became mandatory for employers to offer the 401(k) option to their employees, who then have the option to accept it or not. Hence, there's a possibility that the company you work for does not offer any sort of defined benefit plan partly because of its having made available the 401(k) option.

The biggest disadvantage of a defined benefit plan is that it offers limited opportunity for substantial growth. Because the benefit is simply based on a pre-existing formula, it is therefore not the same as a retirement savings account that could incur return on assets.

At the very least, you can think of a defined benefit plan as a form of annuity which can serve as an emergency buffer fund in case you suddenly run low on retirement income and on any savings and interest earned by your defined contribution plans. It would be prudent to open an IRA with any accredited institution so that you will be guaranteed of at least some return on assets in case you avail of a defined benefit plan instead of a defined contribution plan like a 401(k).

Defined contribution and defined benefit plans are just the most basic means of helping you set up and maintain a retirement fund. This is because they are made readily available to you while you are still working. However, they are not your only options, so don't rely on them to carry the burden on their own.

CHAPTER 4

RETIREMENT-FRIENDLY INVESTING

As soon as you come up with your retirement savings target figure, you'll likely find that the total of your disposable income and the principal amounts of your defined contribution and/or defined benefit plans as well as any earnings generated by those same plans will still fall short of your target. This is sure to happen if you picture yourself living your retirement by traveling a lot, buying things you didn't have time for when you were younger, and spending more on health care and other necessities than you ever did before. The problem is compounded further if you are just a few short years away from retiring from work but you are not enrolled in a retirement savings account such as a 401(k) or an IRA and hence have nothing to rely on but your actual savings in the bank.

Instead of letting your money stay idle, you can use some of it on assets that could potentially earn you more money without you having to do anything other than to keep track of your investments' performance and make sound decisions at all times. This way, as a retired professional, you can still enjoy a steady stream of income without rendering long hours at the office or wherever it is you used to work.

Investing in assets is an option that is open to older retirees as there is no age limit to participating. However, younger people are highly encouraged to also avail of some of these instruments themselves to augment—or possibly even replace—their main source of monthly income. If you make good decisions regarding your investments at the right times, you could make a lot of money while you are still young and perhaps even retire earlier than you originally intended.

Income-generating assets that every future retiree needs to consider

The assets you could choose from are not limited to only one way of generating more money. Some allow you to profit from trading while others incur interest over time, thus allowing you some degree of flexibility when it comes to how your retirement savings are handled. There really is no limit as to how many of each asset type you may own, and in most cases, there will be financial advisors and other professionals who can help you get the most out of your investments.

Here is a rundown of the types of assets you should think about investing in if you want a much bigger nest egg by the time you are no longer part of the workforce.

1. Publicly Traded Stocks

A publicly traded share of stock gives you a portion in the ownership of a private company. However, simply owning shares of stock is not going to yield you any income. You need to be active in stock trading if you are to enjoy any real return on your investment.

Stock trading simply means buying and selling of publicly listed stocks in a stock exchange. You buy stocks to own a bigger portion of a given company and you sell stocks at a profit to earn income from giving up your portion of ownership. The money that you can potentially make from selling stocks could serve as a steady source of income. All you need to achieve this are a computer, an internet connection, access to stock market news and developments, and a high tolerance for risk, as will be explained later.

Stock prices are not fixed at a certain number. Regular trading can push prices upward as sellers can dictate the price in case the demand for a certain stock increases. Moreover, there are regulating bodies that keep a close eye on price movements to make sure there are no sudden price spikes caused by sellers hoping to take advantage of unwitting buyers. Thus, you are guaranteed that price movements are controlled and that no one will be cheating you of your hard-earned money. Many publicly traded stocks also pay out regular dividends to shareholders, thus further increasing the money you earn from your investment.

The actual act of trading is done by a broker, who earns a commission from every transaction they make in your behalf. They know how the market behaves so they have a good idea of when it would be the right time to buy or sell. You can trust your broker to be upfront with you when it comes to what your portfolio should look like; after all, they won't make any money unless they help you make more money.

The caveat of stock trading is that it is not always going to yield you any significant returns. In fact, there could be instances when you'll be forced to sell at a loss, i.e. sell stocks for much less than the price at which you bought them. The stock market is so volatile due to a number of factors that the prices of certain stocks that seem to be performing well can take a huge dive before the end of the trading day. On the other hand, price spikes can occur just as quickly with the potential of turning ordinary people into millionaires virtually overnight, though such events do not happen as often as you might think.

Stock trading requires a high tolerance for risk because you could either gain or lose a lot of money in the blink of an eye. Thus, you can opt to be more conservative in your trading and start with the minimum allowable lots of only a few companies from unrelated industries. Through this option, you get a feel of how stock trading works and you keep any losses you incur as low as possible.

However, great risk often accompanies great reward. You can choose to put in more money than what most people feel comfortable investing if you wish to enjoy significant returns without having to wait several years, though this is only if your stocks keep doing well over time. It could easily go the other way, but you can simply leave your stocks untouched and wait until they recover, or you can sell them as soon as they begin showing signs of decline in order to cut your losses. It is imperative that you have other lucrative investments that you can focus on while waiting for the right opportunity to begin stock trading again.

2. Bonds

A bond is a type of fixed-income security, which means it is guaranteed to earn interest over time— though the rate of interest will not always stay the same—and to give a payout of the principal plus interest upon maturity. In this type of investment, the person or entity who bought a bond from an issuer is given an asset which at the same time is a debt from the point of view of the issuer. The interest that is earned by the bond and given to the bond owner along with the principal upon maturity is essentially the issuer's way of compensating the owner for lending them money.

A bond may be issued by a private company or the government. Unlike shares of stock, a bond cannot be traded openly through an exchange as this does not grant whoever holds the bond a portion in the ownership of the organization that issued it. It is more like an agreement that states that you lent money to an organization that needed it and that they will give all of it back to you plus a little something extra at a later time.

Although bonds are guaranteed to earn interest, the return is much lower than what you could potentially earn from stock trading. Also, any gains generated from stock trading may be withdrawn at any time whereas bonds need to have matured before any payouts could be made by the issuing entities. However, the promise of a guaranteed return on one's investment is too good to simply pass up, and so any retiree who does not want their savings to stay idle would be making a wise financial decision by putting at least some of their money in bonds.

3.   Mutual Funds

Also known as an exchange traded fund, a mutual fund is an investment vehicle that consists of money collected from different investors and invested in a mix of equity (e.g. stocks), fixed-income securities (e.g. bonds and money market instruments), and other tradable assets. All the money that goes into the fund is entrusted to a fund manager who then invests it accordingly to generate gains on capital. These gains (less any commission that the fund manager receives for their work) are then paid out to those who contributed to the fund, and the amount of payout that each investor receives will be proportional to the amount that they put in. Gains can form part of your retirement income so long as the principal you contributed is not withdrawn at any time.

Both potential and current retirees are advised to invest in these two types of mutual funds:

a. *Retirement Income Funds* are mutual funds that are focused on generating moderate growth for any assets whose returns are to be used purely for retirement purposes (e.g. IRAs). Unlike traditional mutual funds that also invest in securities with varying returns and varying corresponding risk, retirement income funds guarantee greater asset value security by investing only in securities with conservative returns. This is an ideal option for people who admit to having low risk tolerance when investing.

b. *Dividend Income Funds* invest only in stocks that periodically pay dividends regardless of their market performance, and these dividends can serve as a steady source of income during one's retirement. However, potential investors are advised that the amount of each dividend will depend on the stock's prevailing performance at the time the dividend was paid out to shareholders. Hence, if a dividend-paying stock has not been performing well for some time, chances are that stock won't pay any dividends at all until such time that it starts performing well again.

4. Index Funds

An index fund is just like a mutual fund in that the money invested in it is in turn used to acquire ownership of stocks, bonds, or any other tradable assets. However, what makes an index fund different from a mutual fund is that the former's portfolio is designed in such a way that it mimics a known lineup of assets used for gauging overall market performance. This lineup is called a market index, examples of which include the Dow Jones Industrial Average and the S&P 500.

The logic behind index funds is that they are intended to represent the entire market by having a portfolio of stocks of a limited number of well-known companies from different business sectors. These stocks are chosen partly because their collective performance is an indicator of the performance of the market as a whole. Investing in an index fund in effect gives you partial (albeit indirect) ownership of some of today's biggest publicly listed companies.

You don't need to pick any stocks yourself since that part has already been done for you. However, this is also perceived as a downside since the portfolio is limited to just a few specific stocks whose collective performance is more or less in sync with that of the market. On the other hand, a mutual fund, through its fund manager, actively trades by buying and selling to ensure the best possible returns regardless of market performance.

Still, no less than American billionaire and investing expert Warren Buffett highly recommends investing in index funds to start building up one's retirement savings. He also recommends investing especially when the market isn't doing well because of the promise of long-term growth even if things look bleak. He supports his statement by citing how the Dow Jones Industrial Average rose from 66 to 11,497 over the course of the previous century, and how the average nearly doubled to 21,000 from the years 2000 to 2017. With this information, it might therefore be wise to at least consider investing some of your savings in index funds as well.

5. Immediate Annuities

An annuity is a type of insurance product wherein the investor is entitled to regular or variable (i.e. made available at any time) payouts over time in exchange for a lump sum contribution. It is not really an investment product that can generate income on top of the principal amount that was put in it. Still, it deserves to be included here since it nonetheless encourages the prudent use of limited available funds as opposed to giving a person a huge sum of money that is likely to be spent without prior careful consideration.

Perhaps the only major drawbacks of annuities are the following:

a. The insurance company that sold you the annuity will require you to pay the lump sum upfront for you to receive payouts later on.

b. The insurance company will impose a hefty fee on you should you decide to withdraw even a portion of that money before the end of the agreed-upon "surrender period," which can last up to ten years from the time you bought the annuity.

Regardless, annuities can still serve as viable "safety nets" so that you will have at least something you could turn to in case you run into some unforeseen expenses such as those for emergency home renovations.

6.   Rental Real Estate

If the idea of having to manage intangible investment vehicles seems somewhat overwhelming, you still have the option to invest in property that you can earn from by renting it out to interested tenants. However, even if you live in a region with a high rental return rate, you will still have to shoulder some of the maintenance expenses, especially if the maintenance issues that arise are not the fault of your tenants.

Remember that managing income property is akin to running a business; it is not an activity through which you can instantly make a lot of money with minimal effort. If you do invest in this option, you can never afford to just sit back and let your money work for you (as is the case with investment vehicles). If you can afford it, you can hire someone who will manage the property full-time to relieve you of much of the physical work involved, but all the important decisions regarding the property still need to be made by you.

The value of diversification

Financial experts recommend not investing all of your disposable income in just one type of asset. Otherwise, you run the risk of putting all of it in just one investment that happens to generate only minimal return or no return at all (as in the case of shares of stock whose price has gone far below that at which you initially bought them), leaving you well short of your targeted retirement income.

Remember not to put all your eggs in one basket. You should diversify your asset portfolio to spread the risk and to enjoy a greater likelihood of capital gain. The question now is, how do you go about it?

Asset allocation strategies you may use

There is no hard and fast rule when it comes to what your portfolio should look like. It's your money that you will be investing anyway, so that means you are free to decide how much of it you will put in a particular asset. However, if you're having trouble deciding where your disposable income should go, you might want to consider these portfolio mixes as suggested by some seasoned financial planners. Note that the percentages are the proportions of principal asset values relative to total fund value.

- Moderate

    o 60% stocks

    o 35% fixed income

    o 5% cash investments (i.e. short-term assets with maturities of only 90 days or less for each)

This is ideal for those who want substantial asset growth with fund stability being only secondary. They are confident they can handle the volatility of the stock market without getting too excited or anxious and in turn make rash decisions. Thus, they have no problem investing much of their savings in stocks whose potential for growth is much greater than those of other assets even though price increase is not always guaranteed.

- Moderately Conservative

  o 40% stocks

  o 50% fixed income

  o 10% cash investments

This portfolio mix is for those who want to be assured of income and stability without much effort on their part but still want enough stock investments to be able to generate some growth from time to time. As such, the bulk of the portfolio consists of assets whose principal amounts remain intact and whose generated returns are smaller than what stocks can ideally provide. If you want to be aggressive in stock trading for the sake of potential returns but you still want to retain a sizable portion of your fund in assets that guarantee stability, this allocation approach may be the solution you need.

- Conservative

  o 20% stocks

  o 50% fixed income

  o 30% cash investments

As you get older, you are likely to become more concerned about protecting whatever assets you have and less concerned about increasing their value further (assuming you were able to successfully achieve the latter during your earlier years). You may continue to allot half of your portfolio for fixed-income securities while increasing your stake in cash investments, thereby reducing your stock investments. This way, you get the same asset stability that you would enjoy from maintaining a moderately conservative portfolio, but your fund's ability to generate a sizable income within a short period will be severely limited, which is okay in light of your primary goal of preserving your investments.

Final thoughts on investing

You should always treat your investment assets the same way you would treat your house, your car, and all your other possessions. Remember, all these things are in your name, so it is only proper that you treat them with utmost care until the right time to let go of them finally comes. You should always make sound decisions regarding them and never allow your emotions to cloud your judgment. Learn to put your money in those things that can give you peace of mind, not what would cause you to lose sleep over time.

Lastly, don't wait until you're already retired before you start investing. The earlier you start, the more likely it is that you'll have a hefty retirement fund by the time you're about to begin using it.

CHAPTER 5

INVESTING IN YOUR HEALTH

The opening chapter of this book already mentioned that you will begin to spend more money on health care following your retirement (assuming you follow the crowd and opt to retire at 65) than at any other point in your life. This is because your body by that time will have already begun feeling the effects of age catching up, and so you are neither physically nor mentally capable as you were in your twenties, thirties, or even your forties. You will thus need to spend more on essentials including but not limited to multivitamins, nutritional supplements, and prescription medicines for keeping your heart health in check. There will also be the need for emergency health care in case of unexpected illness or injury caused by accidents, which will further cause your medical expenses to skyrocket.

Fortunately, as the years went by, a number of medical breakthroughs, the renewed focus on healthy living, and other factors resulted in an increase in life expectancy among people. All of us now have a greater chance of living longer lives than what some previous generations were able to achieve. Because you are able to live a longer life (provided you take good care of yourself by practicing a healthy lifestyle), you will have more time to truly enjoy your retirement by pretty much doing whatever you want.

However, longer life expectancy doesn't mean you will finally be spared from having to spend on health care after you retire. On the contrary, you could end up spending more on it. The additional years you will be blessed with to enjoy life ironically means additional years of paying for the same health care essentials that were mentioned in the first paragraph of this chapter.

You may choose to withdraw from your retirement savings or from the earnings generated by your investments so that you can properly address this greater need for health care. However, there is no reason for you to resort to this course of action right away. There are a number of options whose sole purpose is to make sure you have at least nearly enough money to cover your emergency medical expenses in the years after you retire.

Investing in your health isn't going to make you wealthier over time, but then again, there is no point in having a sizable retirement fund if you're too sick to use it.

Health care options for retirees

1. Medicare

This is a federal health insurance program open primarily to people aged 65 or older who have been citizens or permanent legal residents of the United States for at least five years. The program is also open to disabled individuals who have been collecting social security for at least two years (such as former military personnel who sustained severe injuries in the line of duty) as well as those who are afflicted with kidney failure and the neuron-destroying condition amyotrophic lateral sclerosis (also known as Lou Gehrig's disease after the famed baseball player who was one of the most notable people ever to be afflicted with it).

Under Original Medicare which was ratified in 1965 are two basic parts, each of which covers a specific range of health care services:

a. *Hospital Insurance (Part A)* involves inpatient hospital confinements, care in skilled nursing facilities, hospice care, and home health.

b. *Medical Insurance (Part B)* covers doctors' services, preventive services (like laboratory and x-ray services), outpatient care, and medical supplies (such as wheelchairs).

Eligible individuals have the option to also avail of prescription drug coverage (Part D) and additional health insurance known as medicare supplement insurance or medigap. The purpose of medigap is to help cover supplemental health care costs such as copayments and deductibles on a per-service basis. It also covers health care availed by US citizens and permanent residents while traveling overseas.

Funding for medicare is provided by the Federal government through the Social Security

Administration. In other words, it is funded by taxpayer dollars. Hence, if you truly want to benefit from medicare when you retire, you should diligently pay your taxes for as long as you are still working.

You contribute tax that is around 1.45% of your salary while your employer pays the same percentage/amount in your name (Self-employed professionals are required to shell out the entire 2.9% themselves.). The deductions might not seem like much, but when you realize that medicare funding was able to constitute a whopping $3.7 trillion or 15% of the Federal budget in 2015, you will see its potential in making basic health care available to a lot of folks who are in need of it.

Despite Federally-funded Original Medicare being the standard health care insurance option for the elderly since 1965, people have come to clamor for a more comprehensive and streamlined package for their needs. This resulted in the introduction of the privately-funded Medicare Advantage Plan (Medicare Part C) which offers the same coverage as Medicare Parts A and B but with some additional benefits. For one, Medicare Advantage already includes Medicare Part D (prescription drug coverage) which could only be availed of separately by a patient who is enrolled in Original Medicare. It also provided vision, hearing, and dental benefits which are not covered by Medicare Part A or B.

Whereas you paid for Original Medicare by taking out 1.45% from your salary regardless of how much you were earning and then paid for your other health care expenses through medigap, Medicare Advantage sets a limit on the maximum amount that you can contribute to the plan. The maximum limit or cap ranges from $3,000 to $6,700 depending on the private health care provider, but paying this amount will already entitle you to the services and other benefits covered by the plan without the need for copayments or deductibles.

Despite the Medicare Advantage name, the program ironically does have some disadvantages. Only a few provider networks offer it, in turn limiting your options, whereas Original Medicare may be availed from major medical centers throughout the country. Also, before your plan will pay for your treatment or any other health care services that you require, your doctor must first provide them with proof that such a procedure is indeed necessary. This restriction seeks to keep costs within budget, but the time you spend explaining your case to your health care provider could have been time spent actually availing of the procedure which will in turn hasten your recovery.

Whichever medicare plan you sign up for will definitely make an impact on your finances because of the costs involved, so learn to choose wisely even before you finally start availing of either option.

2.   Health Insurance Marketplace

For those who voluntarily retire early from the workforce, they will obviously not be entitled to medicare until they reach the age of 65. Fortunately, they can still avail of health coverage after choosing from a wide variety of insurance packages made available by the health insurance marketplace in their state of residence (at least unless the Affordable Care Act or "Obamacare" legislation that requires such state-run marketplaces somehow gets repealed).

Most retiree insurance packages offered by employers require signing up for Original Medicare even before the period for eligibility begins. This is partly because the benefits to which you are entitled under such packages become available only after you become eligible to finally use medicare. If you retire even before you become eligible, the health insurance marketplace will still provide you with options. Otherwise, if you choose not to avail of health insurance despite being able to afford it, you must pay a penalty in the form of an individual shared responsibility payment for every year that you don't have coverage. This penalty is paid when you file your income tax return.

The good news is that the marketplace can help narrow down your choices only to packages that you can afford. The premium you pay will depend on your income, and you can even enjoy a much lower premium if you have dependents, typically your spouse and those among your children who are still minors.

3. Direct Primary Care

Under this model, there is no intervening insurance company that will dictate to you which health care provider you should go to for consultation or treatment of routine cases. You pay a flat monthly subscription to a primary care clinic that employs doctors, nurses, and other health care staff. That subscription already entitles you to avail of their services at no extra charge whereas some insurance companies will charge you even for just *seeing* a doctor.

It's not just the reduced costs that people love about direct primary care. There is also greater doctor-patient interaction due mainly to the higher doctor-to-patient ratio. Since doctors have fewer patients to accommodate, they become more familiar with the medical history of each person that sees them regularly. They can then suggest effective remedies tailored to each patient's needs instead of simply dispensing one-size-fits-all prescriptions that are of very little help.

However, it is only primary care that is provided by such facilities. That includes only clinical visits, house calls, and medication. For hospital stays, surgical procedures, and other forms of secondary and tertiary health care, you may be compelled to consult with an insurance-designated provider of such services. At the very least, direct primary care can help you avoid insurance costs that normally come with consultations and other basic medical services. With the philosophy of an ounce of prevention being worth a pound of cure, you certainly wouldn't complain if that ounce didn't have to charge you anything extra.

4. Health Care Sharing Ministries

These are nonprofit organizations whose members voluntarily shoulder each other's medical bills as an alternative to paying for traditional insurance. Membership in such groups often requires adoption of a specific set of beliefs. Many of these groups accept only practicing Christians (often of the same denomination as that of the group's founders or leaders) while some are less restricting in that they will welcome just about anyone for as long as he or she supports the idea of religious freedom.

In a health care sharing ministry, the members make equal contributions to the fund and so they are all entitled to equal benefits. Payouts are determined by cash flow and are therefore not always guaranteed. However, a number of people have reported a high level of satisfaction from their being members of such groups. They especially praised the fact that they are given the freedom to look for medical providers and treatment options beyond those that are allowed by traditional health insurance programs. Examples are alternative therapy programs like reiki, chiropractic, and Ayurvedic medicine.

Perhaps the only major drawback of health care sharing is that some groups do not cover treatments and other procedures that are forbidden by their faith. For instance, any procedures related to reproductive health are not likely to be paid for by a ministry that professes to be pro-life.

Some parting thoughts on securing health care

Your own health should be among your primary concerns when you are planning for your retirement.

You should thus start thinking about how and where you can avail of health care in the future so that you will spend less time worrying about cost and more time getting the treatment you need.

CHAPTER 6

WHERE YOU CAN SPEND YOUR RETIREMENT

No one ever said that being retired requires you to stay put where you are right now. It's likely that one of the reasons you live where you currently are is that it is not too far from where you work. But once you're no longer working, will you have any other reason to stay there?

You could choose to spend most of your remaining years in your current community since you probably already know just about everyone there and you are contented with what the place has to offer. But if you're feeling somewhat adventurous, if you've always wanted to do other things, and if you believe that all the money that you saved up for your retirement should be well-spent, perhaps moving to another community can bring you closer to what you're looking for.

It might please you to know that there are places not only within the country but also elsewhere around the world that are conducive for living in retirement. Relocating alone will be costly especially if you choose to live overseas, but it will be worth it in light of what you will get after having set foot in your new hometown. So don't be afraid to take that big step especially if it will guarantee you a comfortable life after working full-time.

Retiree-friendly hometown essentials

At this point, you may be wondering what exactly makes a specific area "retiree-friendly." Below are the most important things that retirees look for in a new place of residence:

- Pleasant year-round climate

Be honest; you were never really crazy about watering your lawn in July, raking leaves in November, and shoveling snow in January. Do you still want to spend your years in retirement doing those same chores again and again? Or would you rather live in a place where the weather for most of the year is so pleasant that doing those chores won't be necessary? The climate should be pleasant enough that you will be comfortable however you choose to spend your day, whether outdoors or at home.

- Easy access to basic social services

Living life as a retired working professional is all about convenience. Specifically, you will want to easily avail of basic social services such as health care, public transport, and legal assistance wherever you may be even if these things don't come for free. If you are going to spend years living in a particular area, you first have to make sure you don't need to jump through any hoops just to be able to avail of those services. You're retired and not getting any younger; the last thing you need is having to face and overcome obstacle after obstacle just to benefit from the things that promise to make your life easier.

- Few tax restrictions

You cannot ignore your duty to pay the necessary taxes in the place where you live, but as a retiree, you would still want to preserve as much of your disposable income as you possibly can. This is so that you'll have enough funds to travel every once in a while (No one's stopping you from going wherever you like even after you have permanently relocated.), buy stuff you've always wanted, or pursue hobbies and other leisurely activities you didn't have time for before because you were busy making a living. Living in a place with few tax restrictions means you will be able to truly enjoy the remaining years of your life while still adequately fulfilling your obligation as a resident.

- Low cost of living

You save up for your retirement mainly because you still want to be able to afford both the things you need and want even when you're no longer performing any backbreaking or mentally exhausting work. You have a better chance of achieving this in a place where pretty much everything you buy costs less than in your previous hometown. However, places where the cost of living is higher than the national average or even that of your hometown should not be immediately discarded. A higher cost of living could be a sign of a strong local economy with better infrastructure, more modern facilities, and safer neighborhoods.

- Opportunities for recreation and other worthwhile pursuits

Life isn't always about making more money. In other words, you cannot really enjoy your retirement unless you are able to do the things you love from time to time. You've worked hard your whole life just to get to this point, and so you deserve to have more time doing something that you enjoy even if it won't make you richer. It could be a hobby, a sport, volunteer work, or any other activity that gives you a feeling of fulfillment. After all, your goal here is to be happier, not wealthier.

- Friendly locals

Adjusting to life in a new place of residence can be difficult, especially if you do not personally know anyone there who has been through what you're just starting out to do. However, if the people in that area are known for their welcoming, cordial attitude towards new arrivals, it will make you feel as if you never really left home. When you're still new in town, you could easily find the nearest hospital, church, supermarket, or park or how to get to where you need to go if everyone you come across—whether it's your next-door neighbor, a shop clerk, the garbage collector, or a police officer—will be happy enough to point you in the right direction.

Should you choose to relocate to another country, you will of course prioritize those whose residents have no trouble living with expatriates among them. You would also want to live in a place where English is understood by the locals even if it is not their official language so as to more easily know your way around. It also wouldn't hurt if you exert effort to learn the local language; the people there will certainly appreciate you more for going the extra mile in communicating with them.

Here are some suggestions on where you could relocate and spend your later years with as few hassles as possible. Please note that some of the places featured here get passing marks in some of the criteria mentioned above but not in others. Also included are details on what makes each place unique.

5 retiree-friendly places in the United States (in alphabetical order)

Unless you have lived in even just one of the cities in this list, you might want to know more about why you should consider relocating there.

1. Beaufort, South Carolina

This small city of only 13,000 nonetheless has a very strong local economy driven mainly by tourism. Retirees will definitely enjoy the ample opportunities that Beaufort provides for golf and fishing. However, they might also find the city's "old town" charm a good enough reason for them to stay here for the long term.

It might do you well to know as early as now that Beaufort is also home to a sprawling military airbase, so don't be surprised if you suddenly hear high-speed jet planes and helicopters getting closer and closer until they're finally right over your head. Those are just Beaufort-based US Marine Corps aviation units conducting some much-needed training before they are sent overseas.

2. Franklin, Tennessee

This little-known suburb of Nashville provides retirees excellent yet highly affordable health care and a cost of living lower than the national average. It also boasts of one of the lowest crime rates of any American city; crime statistical data for 2014 provided by the FBI revealed zero homicides and just five robbery incidents in Franklin during that year.

Retirees who choose to reside in Franklin can benefit from zero state income taxes. However, dividends and investment income will still be taxed, so keep this in mind if much of what goes into your retirement fund will come from your investments.

3. Prescott, Arizona

Arizona isn't all arid desert. There are actually retiree-friendly cities and towns all throughout. The city of Prescott smack-dab in the middle of America's 48th state is a notable example, boasting of financial perks that retirees are sure to love such as low state income tax rates and tax-free social security. There are also golf courses and hiking trails for those who want to remain physically active during their retirement as well as museums, galleries, theaters, and various yearly festivals for those who are more into arts and entertainment.

Lastly, Prescott is located in Yavapai Country, which experiences lower summer temperatures compared to elsewhere in the southern part of the state. If you've always wanted to visit or perhaps even move to Arizona but are having second thoughts because of the climate throughout the state, Prescott is something of a welcome exception.

4. Salt Lake City, Utah

Although the cost of living in Salt Lake City is higher than the national average and that social security benefits here are taxed, the capital of Utah is nonetheless favored by retirees for its clean air, efficient public transport, and vibrant downtown atmosphere. There are also plenty of golf courses, but if you don't mind the cold, the city also provides opportunities for winter sports as it is located right at the foot of the Wasatch and Oquirrh mountain ranges.

Health care costs in Salt Lake City are slightly above the national average. However, the city enjoys a high doctor-to-patient ratio, which means retirees are more likely to benefit from adequate treatment here compared to many other American cities.

5. Venice, Florida

Just like the world-famous city of Venice in Italy, this Florida community is noted for its numerous canals and for its buildings whose designs were inspired by Italian Renaissance architecture. It also has a wide array of parks, beaches, tennis courts, and golf courses.

Venice prides itself on its cost of living being lower than the national average, affordable health care, low crime rates, and warm year-round climate. Somewhat surprisingly, more than half of the city's population are aged 65 and older, which implies that living here is highly advantageous for elderly retirees.

5 retiree-friendly countries (in alphabetical order)

1. Costa Rica

This Latin American country is popular among retirees who are originally from the US because of its many beaches, friendly locals, the low cost of living, pleasant climate, and modern (and very affordable) health care. If you are an older retiree and you decide to relocate to Costa Rica, you could qualify for one of the government-managed health care systems that are partnered with numerous hospitals and clinics throughout the country. Paying a monthly subscription fee based on your income will automatically entitle you to whatever treatment or procedures you need without having to shell out additional money.

You also have the option to avail of the services of private health care providers. Although this could cost you more than if you availed of government-run health care, you can still expect to pay much less than what these same services would cost in the US.

2. Malaysia

This Southeast Asian country is a popular retiree destination because of its warm tropical climate, its rich culture, the low cost of living, and its efficient public transport system. English isn't a commonly spoken language here though it is widely understood by many of the locals. Thus, you won't have much difficulty asking people for help in getting around.

Malaysia also excels in the area of health care. The country's doctors, many of whom completed their medical studies in the US and Britain, are among the best in the region. Medical costs are also lower than those of the US. For example, a complete package that includes initial consultation, diagnosis, surgery, and a private hospital room could cost around $2,000 whereas a similarly configured package could fetch up to ten times as much in the US.

Lastly, Malaysia is ideal for those who love to travel in light of its being a strategically located transport hub. You could easily fly to other destinations in Asia from any of the country's four major international airports, all of which are hubs of some well-known low-cost airlines.

3. Malta

This small island country situated in the middle of the Mediterranean Sea boasts of pleasant weather for ten months in a year, the low cost of living compared to that of the United States (i.e. monthly expenses going no higher than $2,700), and opportunities for watersports such as sailing, snorkeling, and diving. Malta is so small in area that you can easily get around by public transport alone. Thus, there is no need for you to own a car while you are living there.

Health care in Malta is exceptional, and it is made more attractive by medical costs being much lower than in the US. However, even with insurance being affordable, you could easily pay for medication and doctor visits out of your own pocket.

4. Mexico

Mexico has also proven to be a favorite destination among American retirees. First of all, it is just south of the US, making relocation easier in terms of the logistics involved. Spending just $1,200 a month can give you everything you need and more. The climate also varies by area, which means you can live someplace cooler without having to leave the country.

Expat retirees aged 60 or older can even qualify for senior citizen discount cards. These entitle holders to discounts of up to 10% on such things as airline and bus tickets, medical procedures, hotel reservations, and groceries.

While it is true that Mexico has been getting some bad publicity because of crime, such incidences are limited to only a few areas. It's a big country anyway, and there are places where expats can live without worrying about their safety, such as the Lake Chapala and Riviera Maya communities in the southern and eastern portions.

5. Portugal

Portugal offers a generally mild climate, low cost of living peaking at only $2,200 per month, convenient public transport, low crime rate, and good food. The country is known for its seafood, which is ideal for older retirees who are restricted to high-protein low-calorie diets.

Portugal also has a wide selection of entertainment centers, beaches, and golf courses, giving retirees plenty of options with regards to how and where they can spend their free time.

Of course, these lists are not exhaustive as there are plenty of other retiree-friendly places in the United States and elsewhere around the world that are not featured here. Also, time and circumstances can mean that other places that used to be virtually unknown can later on become veritable retirement havens. You can always perform additional research on which other destinations will qualify as retiree-friendly now that you know what to look for in what will be your home when you are no longer part of the workforce.

Remember that you are always free to relocate again in case you do not see yourself truly being happy while living in the place you initially chose as your new hometown when you retire. You could even go back to where you lived while you were still working if you feel it will be a better move for you. After all, you can never truly enjoy your retirement in a place that gives you nothing but stress when it's supposed to make it easy for you to live the rest of your days in peace and comfort.

CHAPTER 7

A BRIEF GUIDE FOR THE
LATE STARTER

Are you planning for your retirement but you don't have that much time left because you started planning much later than you're supposed to? It's highly likely that you are only starting now because you've just realized that you have not set aside enough money to give yourself a source of funds for a time when you will no longer be receiving a steady paycheck.

You are not alone. In a survey conducted by banking rate comparison website GOBankingRates.com in 2016, 23% of the respondents admitted to having saved less than $10,000 for their retirement while a third of the respondents reported that they have not saved anything at all. This is a rather alarming piece of news as it means a lot of people still do not realize the importance of retirement planning, especially doing it well before retirement.

All is not lost, though, for a number of financial planning experts believe that you can still build up a reasonable retirement fund even with very little time remaining. The resulting amount might not be big enough to buy you your dream car or house, but it's better than having only a measly amount in your name when you retire.

Here are some tips on how you can save up for your retirement if it is just around the corner. Even if your current employer is gracious enough to allow you to be on their payroll even after you turn 65, in which case you have no choice but to postpone your retirement to a later time, implementing these actions as early as you can will still give you a reasonable amount of savings you could fall back on in your later years.

Tip #1: Save, save, save

Every penny of your disposable income that you would otherwise spend on things that don't ensure asset growth should go into a separate savings account that you can withdraw from only when you retire. Until then, you should make sure this seemingly miniscule fund keeps on growing. That means making such sacrifices as going on only one or two vacations every year, downsizing to a less expensive house and car to further reduce your usual necessary expenses, and even giving up simple pleasures like that tall latte you used to buy every other day at the coffee shop just outside your office. You may even need to apply for a job on the side, even one with lower pay, just to help speed up the growth of your savings.

Increasing your savings will also mean getting rid of your credit cards. With the way interest rates are now, the convenience you get from not having to carry a lot of cash with you wherever you go isn't worth the additional expense. What you would otherwise use to pay off interest and other related fees can instead go into your savings for you to spend on more important things later on.

Tip #2: Don't take on more risk

There's a huge temptation among late starters to invest purely in high-return assets such as stocks as a way of making up for lost time. The potential for significant returns is indeed high, but the potential for losses is even higher. You should instead adopt an asset allocation strategy wherein the bulk of your portfolio is in low-risk fixed-income securities and cash investments that nonetheless guarantee some returns over time since you will be more concerned with preserving your principal than with making your fund value grow significantly. It would be better for you to build your savings up little by little than to boldly take huge steps and possibly end up faring no better than when you started.

Tip #3: Open a Roth IRA

In Chapter 3 of this book, you already learned about individual retirement accounts and their advantages over the 401(k) plan. Just to recap, an IRA will eventually pay you back all the contributions you put into it plus interest when you retire. Roth IRAs have the added benefit of tax-free withdrawals since any contributions you made to the account have already been taxed, hence allowing you to get your money back without having to pay Uncle Sam.

You can easily open a Roth IRA even when you're close to retiring as the maximum age limit for opening this type of retirement account is seventy and a half. You can keep contributing to it even after you retire for as long as you are earning steady income that was incurred through legitimate means, like returns on your assets or a part-time post-retirement job that doesn't pay as much as what you were earning before. The money you save from cutting down on unnecessary purchases and expenses (as discussed in tip #1 earlier) can even go directly into this fund.

The $6,000 maximum yearly contribution limit imposed on people aged 50 and above will likely yield only $310,000 after 20 years, and unsurprisingly, the yield is even lower for those who are unable to max out their contributions. Nonetheless, this option allows you to slowly build your retirement savings up into something that could take care of many of your daily living expenses provided you continue the habit of spending only on the things you need.

Tip #4: Set aside enough for insurance

Just because you started planning for your retirement late doesn't mean you can already skimp on some of the essentials. You will still need insurance to cover expenses relating to your health and your property. Life insurance is another option you need to consider, especially if your children are still young enough to qualify as dependents in the first few years following your retirement.

Some final thoughts on starting late

Saving up for your retirement is challenging whether you have several or just a few years remaining before you finally leave the workforce. However, setting aside even a little each day can make a difference later on, so don't put it off until tomorrow. No matter how old you are, you should start saving up today!

CONCLUSION

I hope that this book was able to teach you the value of early planning for your eventual retirement from the workforce upon or before reaching old age.

By now, you will have already realized that preparing for retirement is no walk in the park. It involves constant planning, reassessing, and implementation of action to ensure a favorable outcome. You have a much better chance of achieving your goals and committing fewer mistakes if you devote much of your free time to this necessary activity while you are still a young working professional.

The next step is to apply what you have learned from this book and start preparing for your own retirement. You could even share what you've learned with others, especially those are still not sold on the importance of planning ahead.

May all your efforts in this endeavor be rewarded by a comfortable life wherein you can afford the things you need even if you have stopped working as a full-time professional.

Finally, if you enjoyed this book, then I'd like to ask you for a favor. Leaving a review on Amazon is one of the best and easiest ways to support self-published authors.

Thank you and good luck!

www.ingramcontent.com/pod-product-compliance
Lightning Source LLC
Chambersburg PA
CBHW071222220526

45468CB00002B/702